A One-Sided Coin

Jim Metcalf

Published by James Metcalf, 2022.

A ONE-SIDED COIN

First edition. July 1, 2022.

ISBN: 979-8201482008

Written by Jim Metcalf.

Table of Contents

This memoir is dedicated to Sandra Leeman Metcalf, my love and companion for sixty-three years along with our family.

Our daughter Patricia and her husband Dan along with their three children Sarah, Leilani and Brian.

Our Son Timothy and his wife Jennifer with their three children Sophia, Alexander and Colette.

Introduction

I have been awaiting this day all week like a kid waiting for Christmas. Today, I am happy to be attending a church service for All Saints Day, a time to remember those loved ones who have died but not before making a major impact on our lives. I am praying for my love and lighting a candle of remembrance of a lifetime of experiences we had together. My feelings today are very happy and close to those I had so many years ago when we stood here in this same church with our family and friends exchanging marriage vows. This church is Trinity Episcopal where Sandy and I were married on August 3, 1963, beginning fifty-five years of a loving, happy relationship.

We moved away from this town and this church. But now almost sixty years later I am so happy to be here in this same place to able to express my love for my wife. I never thought that I would ever survive the pain, anger, devastation, darkness and loneliness of losing the love of my life from the time we were kids. I felt that my life had ended with Sandy's passing. Since we lived and breathed our lives together, how would I survive alone in this hurricane of devastation?

Haruki Murakami wrote, "And once the storm is over you won't remember how you made it through, how you managed to survive. You won't even be sure, in fact, whether the storm is really over. But, one thing is certain. When you come out of the storm, you won't be the same person who walked in."

1

I will never forget the painful, empty silence following Sandy's last breath. It was like I was thrown into a vacuum where no sense of time, space and feelings exist. She was lying on the bed in the hospice motioning me to massage her right knee. She had hurt it years ago as a result of a fall in the office where she worked but never wanted to report it for fear of angering the owner. I continued to softly massage that knee as the only thing that gave her comfort. I kept telling her that I loved her and asking what else could I do to make her comfortable. There was no answer except her hand holding on to mine.

Sandy's breathing was very shallow, seeming like every breath was an effort. Then she stopped for a second, took a deep breath, and she was gone. That was the last breath of sixty-three years of loving togetherness. It was surreal. We had been together like a two-sided coin since we were fourteen. How could it end like this? How could our life end with one last breath? A one-sided coin is useless. I felt like I had died with her. I kept telling her that I loved her and would see her soon, but I was probably just talking to the wind.

There was an explosive rage inside me. I began identifying and blaming everyone who I thought did not take Sandy seriously during her pleas for help. I started to remember every person who acted like they were just doing their job without caring. It didn't matter if Sandy was a mannequin, a person, or a sack of potatoes; the treatment had the same objective distance; finish with this one and on to the next. The technician who took her mammogram a year after breast cancer treatment and who, way out of line, announced, "Wow, you better get this checked." The clergy who was getting ready for a new job so did not have time to visit Sandy during her illness, even though she had been a member of the church for half a century including performing the role of treasurer of the women's group. Her personal physician who explained Sandy's fatigue by saying, "You're old and old people get tired."

I had run a psychiatric facility for adolescents where we all cried every time a kid came in from being raped, tortured or banged up from a failed suicide attempt. To me, care is a personal investment, not a manila folder with a name and a snapshot so the clinician could mispronounce a name of the person in the snapshot. I figured that every one of those white-jacketed house staff who did not see a very sick woman but rather a body of data to apply to an algorithm must have a fear of interacting with people. Would these mechanics treat their mother this robotically? I could not stand this indifference from those in the hospital and those in the hospice. Didn't anyone realize that Sandy was a living, breathing person with seventy-seven years of a beautiful life? She deserved more than being represented by a number and list of diagnostic presentations.

I yelled at one neurologist who was using Sandy as a prop to have a resident practice doing a spinal tap. When I asked him to explain he said that the resident had to learn. But not on my wife, without even talking to her or asking her permission. Then there was the junior oncologist on Memorial Day weekend complaining that the senior staff left the bad news of moving to hospice to him. Poor baby. He must have missed that part of training about doctors having to care for people.

I cannot say all were uncaring. The hospital nursing staff were great and very supportive. They understood the anxiety of a family with a very sick member. Throughout their training and career, the bad news explanations, clean up and blame were most times dumped on them. When I discovered that a meal of pot roast was being served with plastic utensils, I asked the charge nurse to send me the dietary manager when she came on the floor. Nursing staff said this happens all the time, especially on nights and weekends, and nurses must run from room to room cutting up food for patients because the plastic utensils break easily. A dietary supervisor came to the floor to explain the situation by saying that the dishwashers throw many of the metal utensils into the trash when cleaning the trays so plastic utensils are used on off shifts. I came close to exploding by asking her if she could eat a meat entrée with plastic utensils.

After that the nurses wanted to bring me more issues they had to deal with and actually told me that I might want to meet the hospital administrator and director of nurses when they made administrative rounds. It was a mistake for those two happy souls to stop by and ask how we were enjoying our stay. What the hell did they think, this was a Holiday Inn? I told them the story of plastic silverware and the story about the parking garage gates not working on weekends when parking attendants were off. The floor staff listened in, smiling, as they were the ones who had to field all the complaints from patients and families. The nursing supervisor wanted me to handle more problems, but I politely said that I was consumed with my wife's care. They even told the residents not to enter my wife's room for fear of being chewed out. I had trained and worked with a couple of these nurses in another hospital so they became even more supportive of Sandy.

For a few days the house staff under the direction of a fully trained algorithm neurologist tested and talked, talked and tested until their decision tree ran out of branches. Finally, after a suggestion by nursing staff, a brain surgeon was consulted. He met with me and showed me a head scan of what looked like a stage four glioblastoma jelly-like brain tumor. He explained that a biopsy was the only way to confirm the situation. He also said that the jelly-like tumor would be inoperable because it was not confined as a small, hard mass. This surgeon was the perfect example of how close and caring a doc should be. A floor nurse told me that he was the best in the business because he understood the highly emotional nature of operating on someone's brain.

I agreed and he performed a brain biopsy which confirmed the worst-case situation. But this surgeon did not pass the message to the attending doc, instead he came looking for me and we talked in private as he knew that my wife of fifty-five years was going to die in a short time. Of course, the algorithm house staff tried to suggest a move to a Boston hospital for experimental treatment. Thankfully this surgeon explained the facts of life to them, that seventy-seven-year-old people are not appropriate for experiments, so they put away their algorithm iPads and slipped off into hiding. On Memorial Day, the staff arranged our transfer to a local hospice where the oncologist said Sandy would receive comfortable care.

2

I fell in love with Sandy when we were both fourteen-year-old freshmen in high school. She was sitting in study hall when I got thrown out of French class for being a *cul intelligent*. The seat behind her in study hall was open so I took my place looking at the most beautiful jet-black ponytail. In trying to get her attention I played with her ponytail out of sight of the teacher sitting up front. Sandy was quiet and new to the school so did not make a fuss as she should have. She should have yelled or turned around and slapped me, but she was a quiet girl from a small town in Maine who had just moved here with her parents and two younger brothers. It was traumatic for her to be taken out of her ninth-grade class of friends in Maine to be put in our class of strangers here in Massachusetts. I so much wanted to get to know her but our only contact was this study hall. Sandy was in the business program while I was in college prep, undeservedly. So, I began a pattern of getting thrown out of French class two or three times a week when she was in study hall. As one would expect I failed French that year and always jokingly said Sandy was the reason I could not speak French. However, the French teacher finally told me that a *cul intelligent* is a smart ass who should never learn French or any other language.

Both of us were quiet kids, she living on North Street and I on South Street on the opposite side of town so we never really had contact other than study hall. Fortunately, we both went to a high school dance and I finally got up enough nerve to ask Sandy to join me on the floor for a slow dance. It was absolute heaven holding her on the dance floor. I forgot about everything in my life except her. I mumbled some words asking her if I could walk her home. This was the first time we actually talked and both of us did not want the night to end. We walked past her home for about a half mile to the muddy brook bridge. In turning around to head back to her home we kissed for the first time. I was off the ground. I can still remember the feeling of walking home as if I were floating three feet off the ground. I knew that I had found the love of my life.

Earlier that year, I had applied for and was accepted to work a summer job at a camp in New Hampshire, but that was now out of the question as I couldn't leave Sandy. Instead, I became a stock boy at a local grocery store in town. As we both turned fifteen, we started going steady and went to the school prom with an older couple who could drive. We just kept asking them to keep driving around town so we could keep this night going forever. Sometime before sunrise the driver finally told us to get out, as the night was long over for them. We were now going steady and I spent as much time at Sandy's house as her parents could tolerate. They even seemed to adopt me as I took some vacations to Maine with them and went hunting and fishing with Sandy's brothers.

Life was good as I was with my love and we would even talk of marriage in the future. However, we also experienced one of my worst dumb moves and biggest regrets of my life. As we were going steady, I came under excessive harassment from my schoolmates who kept referring to me as "ball and chain" and other derogatory terms suggesting I was not part of their group because I was going steady. The pressure got to be too much so I broke up with her just before our junior prom and took another girl to the prom. I immediately regretted my peer pressured decision. Sandy spent that night with a girlfriend of hers who also did not attend the prom. I spent the entire evening wishing the prom would end quickly as I missed Sandy. Fortunately, she forgave me and we made up, continuing our relationship, but I'll never forget the pain I caused Sandy.

3

We continued going steady through graduation. Sandy wanted to be an accountant, but the guidance person said she should not go to school, but rather enter the workforce as an office clerk because she was in the business program. To try to convince her, he said she was very smart and could work herself up to head clerk someday. Sandy was stubborn and rejected that idea. I really admired her for standing up for herself. This was the 1950's when only the top college prep students were recommended to go on to college with the rest targeted for work in local businesses. Women typically had only four choices: marriage, nursing, teaching or clerking in local offices. Sandy applied to an accounting school where she was accepted as one of two female students. In fact, the second female in her class became Sandy's maid of honor at our wedding. Sandy graduated among the top of her class and in addition, was selected as queen of the senior prom.

I had an uncle who had some connections allowing me to enter a junior college engineering program. I lived in a rooming house then moved in with my aunt and uncle for the remainder of the year. Sandy commuted an hour to school every day with a carload of other students. Sandy and I would see each other on weekends and write a couple of letters to each other during the week. I flunked out due to poor study skills while Sandy excelled, her grades gaining a number of offers after graduation from large banks and insurance companies away from home. I was very proud and envious of her intelligence and always accepted the fact that she was a lot smarter than me.

After my academic failure, I obtained a laborer's job of killing brush on the electric company's power lines, crossing forests, swamps, and mountains. The work was tough as we mixed chemicals into fuel oil and sprayed everything growing under the powerlines. It certainly gave me time to think, and I realized that I didn't want to do this for the rest of my life.

I applied to a four-year local teacher's college and had hopes of attending in the fall, but my high school guidance counselor would not recommend me, saying that I would embarrass the high school due to my lack of academic skills. As a courtesy, the teacher's college to which I applied sent me a letter saying they could not accept me as their quota was filled, but if I wanted to wait a year, they could offer me a seat in their next freshman class. I don't know if they would have actually offered me a seat or hoped that I would just disappear into the working world never to be seen again. That letter was my only chance, so I saved it and showed up a year later, with the letter in hand at the admissions office, saying that I was ready to accept their offer. They reluctantly allowed me in and I began a 4-year program in teacher preparation.

At the beginning of the year of waiting, the electric company offered me a job covering for a meter reader who retired for health reasons. Sandy entered her second year of college and we continued to date throughout this time with my job providing us with money to plan our future together. In 1961 Sandy graduated and gained a good financial position with a manufacturing company. I entered the local teacher's college with the hope of teaching mathematics. Those years were great as Sandy was thought of highly by her company and, with her mentoring, I was successful in college. In 1963 we decided to get married and move into a two-room apartment in Sandy's folks' house. Our life together was truly one of love and enjoyment of each other. Before we got married, we had to decide which church we would join and what religion we would follow. Sandy was raised as a light- duty Methodist who didn't attend church every Sunday. I had no religion due to my folks' difficult, mixed marriage. However, I was secretly baptized a Catholic by my grandmother to give me a path to heaven should I die as an infant.

Sandy and I began having dates on Sunday mornings, attending different churches to see where we were comfortable. We found a small, basement level, Episcopal church named St. Mary's that we both liked. The pastor was an old, retired English Anglican who immediately took us under his grandfatherly wing. He taught us how to follow the religious service then prepared us for confirmation so we could be married in the church. We could not have found a better teacher and advisor. We wanted him to marry us but St. Mary's was a very small basement church with no first floor like most churches. Not a problem for our old Anglican pastor. He had some connection to the Western Massachusetts Episcopal Bishop so we had our choice of churches. On August 3, 1963 we were married by this pastor with pull, in a full-sized Episcopal church in our home town and began a strong marriage thanks to his instruction.

4

Married life was like a dream job. We were not kids anymore. We had responsibilities but we thought about each other twenty-four hours a day and enjoyed spending our time together telling each other what we did when we were apart. We had newly married friends who we met socially to trade stories about the adjustment from being school kids to responsible, married adults. What a great time we all had. We had very little money, but these were the happiest years of our lives. To make a little money I worked as a weekend manager in a Friendly's Sandwich Shop. A wonderful bakery was located next door and I would supply the baker with coffee and food when he started his Sunday night shift making Monday morning's donuts and pastries. When I would close my shop about midnight, he would have a bag of fresh donuts ready for me to share with Sandy at breakfast.

During this time in my life, I began to understand why my French teacher called me a *cul intelligent*, why I'd failed the first year of junior college, and why I did not want to spend my life hauling tanks of fuel oil and chemicals through dense brush. But to burn it into my brain were the drunks that would come into the sandwich shop at closing on Sunday night asking me to make them food which would settle their stomachs so they could make it to work in the mills on Monday morning. These guys were

World War II vets who were productive members of society, but who escaped their personal horrors by spending their weekends in the local VFW and bars. Come Sunday night they knew that in order to keep their factory jobs, they had to show up sober on Monday morning. That's why they came into my sandwich shop and emptied their pockets of what was left of their small paychecks on the counter as a handful of change saying, "Can you make me something to settle my stomach?"

These guys lived with their mothers or in flop houses. If they were married coming back from the war, the booze destroyed those relationships. I loved these guys because they used their own examples to counsel me every Sunday night. I don't know how many times I heard, "Don't be like us. Go to school. Be somebody. Don't drink. Love your wife with your whole heart." It's strange, as often your wisest teachers are those you least expect to teach you a lesson.

The time when I was in college and Sandy was beginning her career was a happy time for us, full of promise. Our families, friends, coworkers and my Sunday night customers all helped to mold our marriage into a oneness where we would rather operate as a partnership than a pair of individuals.

In June of 1965 I graduated from college. Sandy was pregnant with our daughter, Patricia, due on graduation day. During graduation all my classmates would look at me, asking, "Is that your wife?" whenever a moan or noise was heard in the audience. Pat was born a few days later and we started that loving family portion of our lives.

5

During my practice teaching I chose to teach a special needs class. I loved it because the kids were so upbeat and appreciative of efforts to teach them. I decided to obtain extra training and accept a teaching position in secondary special education at a college town in New Hampshire. We could not find an affordable apartment so we took out a loan and purchased a mobile home, locating it across the river in Vermont in a mobile home park. The park was like a little village, mostly made up of young construction workers' families, who stayed close to the Interstate Highway system that was being constructed. The men left early each day to travel to their jobs while the women formed a close-knit group to walk to the local post office for mail or help each other with all types of young family issues. As the accountant, Sandy was always asked about how to stretch a paycheck to cover the expenses we all shared. It was a cold, snowy winter, but between our neighbors and fellow teachers, we really enjoyed our young family lives. One of my fellow teachers belonged to the Dartmouth Outing Club which had cabins along the Appalachian Trail allowing us to rent them for a small fee on weekends. It was great fun when four or five couples and their kids would hike in to a cabin carrying food, bedding, clothing, and coal for the stove to enjoy the winter isolation of the Trail. Our daughter Pat was about eight months old and could fit in the cabin wood box for a crib. It was really terrific sharing the different foods that each brought in, but the surprise came at Sunday morning breakfast before we hiked out to civilization. The standing rule was that Sunday breakfast consisted of all the leftover food which we did not eat. Soups, casseroles, lasagnas, chips and dips along with beer and wine were served, requiring strong stomachs before the march out to our cars.

It did not take long for my new-to-the-school position to become an issue with the administration. Although not part of the initial definition before I accepted the job, the school wanted an isolated class with the windows whitewashed, meals sent in and students walked to the bathrooms together. I did not believe in that type of isolation education so I would negotiate arrangements with regular class teachers to allow my kids into classrooms where they could excel and feel like regular students.

The shop teacher was a friend so he allowed me to bring my class to the woodshop for project work. Perhaps the straw that broke the camel's back was when I encouraged my class to build a crossword puzzle which they submitted to one of the college prep literary magazines and saw it accepted and published with full credit to the class. It was great for the kids but not for me, as the administration did not agree with my methods and failed to renew my contract after the first year. It was a shock, yet the best thing that could happen to my career.

6

At the same time that I was ending my first teaching job the state psychiatric hospital won a large grant to develop an experimental treatment program for inpatient children and adolescents. A special education teacher from a neighboring town was selected to develop the program. He heard about my experience teaching special education and offered me the opportunity to work alongside him in developing this new program. We started with about thirty kids from eight to eighteen years old. Al wanted to work with the younger kids while I enjoyed the teen aged group.

We moved our mobile home to a new under-construction park in Concord. With young and retired families moving into this new park it seemed like every week called for Welcome Wagon introductions. We made such wonderful friends during our park stays in Vermont and New Hampshire. We remained in contact with them throughout our lives.

We were funded for three years to work on this exciting concept of treating an inpatient population of children and adolescents using education as a therapeutic model. We designed a school in the basement of one of the buildings. It contained a gym which meant we could include a number of games and physical activities. I wrote an additional grant for a workshop which we placed in an abandoned kitchen. We began to add staff who would function as teachers but act as therapists. This was nothing fancy as the therapies consisted of personal interest, love, reinforcement of positive behaviors and protection against harm. We had a psychiatrist, psychologist and social worker on staff as most problems touched families, schools and communities. Our treatment team grew to ten that became two volleyball teams to play away the stress at the end of many days.

During this period of our lives our small family grew with the addition of our son Timothy. When Sandy called me to come home because she was in labor, I broke speed records driving home to bring her to the local acute care hospital to experience the delivery of our second child. When we arrived in maternity the floor nurse said that there were five women in labor and one heading into delivery so I was to take charge of one labor room containing Sandy and two other women.

I said, "Are you nuts? What do I know about labor?"

She snapped back saying, "Look, we are overbooked and short-staffed and you work in a hospital so you can watch these three women."

I tried pleading my case saying, "I work in a psychiatric hospital." She replied, "These are all psychiatric hospitals so just call me if you see a baby starting to appear in a bed."

I don't know how many times I asked Sandy and the other two, "Are you alright? Are you alright? Are you alright?" Each of the other two women took turns yelling, "It's time," followed by me yelling for the delivery nurse who calmly wheeled each in turn to delivery. Now it was down to Sandy and me in labor.

All of a sudden, a fire alarm began ringing and I could see fire trucks arriving outside the windows. Sandy got out of bed saying, "I've had it and I'm going home." What do you do when your wife will not listen to your pleading for her to get back in bed? All she said was," You're no labor room nurse so I don't have to listen to you." I start growling, "Look lady, I'm in charge of this labor room and if you don't get back in bed, I'll put you back in bed." Two problems; first, they always keep the labor room beds set high to match to the delivery table and they never lock the wheels for quick trips into delivery. Second, where do you grab a pregnant woman to lift her into bed? I tried holding onto Sandy while chasing her bed around the room, finally catching it in a corner. I then grabbed her low around her hips and lifted her back into bed while listening to some pretty nasty language from her directed at me. My I love you' s meant nothing to this woman I no longer knew. The floor nurse came in saying, "We are ready if she is." Sandy delivered our beautiful son Timothy and I needed to change my shorts from my first and last shift as a labor room nurse despite the floor nurse asking if I would like to work as on-call labor room staff.

We were building such an innovative treatment program that when I approached the university for a master's degree program, they agreed to assemble a unique combination of courses in clinical counseling, family therapy, psychology, criminology and education. My program was called clinical psychiatric counseling with practicums under the direction of psychiatrists. My thesis involved using pre-computer simulation games to measure improved social skills and predict success in society. These elementary games proved useful and after defending my thesis, I was awarded my degree.

During the time developing this program our family and our treatment team became braided together as we were on call for crises twenty-four hours a day and we all socialized often to deal with the stress of the job. When you're dealing with kids who have been beaten, raped, tortured or who have lost reality due to drug use your emotions become raw. We tried to cope with the stress by meeting weekly with a psychiatrist to learn to balance between uncaring rock-hard emotions and completely involved uncontrollable identification with these kids who have been treated in inhuman ways. Our program was successful beyond the most optimistic expectations. Our methods were not rocket science, instead they were based on love, respect, safety and total fun. We built programs with the kids rather than for the kids. Even their school work which was considered a vehicle rather than an outcome grew from one and a half to two grade levels in less than eight weeks. But for all of us on the treatment staff it required an intensive 24/7 commitment and life style. We all were convinced if we applied our methods to normal public-school kids, they would not only achieve at greater speed and accomplish more, but their mental health would be above normal levels.

7

After three years of this intensive life style Sandy and I decided that we needed a career with less stress and intensity to allow more focus on our family relationships. For stress relief, we spent a great deal of time with family in Maine.

When Sandy was a young child, her father enlisted in the Navy early in World War II along with her uncles, all part of the greatest generation. Her father was stationed in Norfolk, Virginia so Sandy's mother joined him as his ship was being prepared for sailing to the Pacific. Sandy was left with her grandmother in Maine for months which thrilled the woman who raised four farm boys and no girls. Sandy's grandmother Lil taught her all the farm chores like gardening, cooking, cleaning, making clothes and enjoying neighbors at grange social events. Grammy Lil also taught and inspired Sandy to be the competent, independent person she became. Grammy Lil told her that there was nothing she couldn't achieve. They formed a close bond which continued throughout Lil's life.

At the end of the war Sandy's father and uncles returned safely to restart their lives. Her uncle Archie owned farm land which bordered a lake so they decided to build three small rental cabins along the shore for tourists and fishermen. The first cabin was built in 1952 and was named Sandra Joan as the practice then was to name cabins after women in the family. Many families including ours stayed in the cabin enjoying the lake out the front door. During the stressful time when we were looking to move on from the psychiatric program, Sandy's uncle Archie gave the Sandra Joan cabin to us as an encouragement to continue our visits and enjoyment of our greater Maine family. This was probably the greatest gift we could have ever received as that cabin was where our son took his first steps on the lake shore and where many family milestones were celebrated. We considered the Sandra Joan cabin a magical place as we could not only relax there but we could contemplate our problems, find peace in tough times and refresh as we began new phases in our life together.

My search for a position identified an acute care hospital in Worcester Massachusetts that had a new administrator with the task of converting this average hospital into a leadership facility within a growing competitive healthcare community. I was hired as director of education with the responsibility to enhance and create training programs which would focus on high quality care in every aspect of a patient's or their family's experience. Nothing was "good enough." Everything from meals and housekeeping to medical, nursing and ancillary care had to focus on the best in class.

I thought the transition would be relatively smooth, but one experience caused me to rethink my new job. One day as I walked through the dietary area of the hospital, I passed a middle aged rather large woman whose job was to clean out the food trucks which were pushed to every floor with hot meals on trays. Just after I passed this woman, I heard her scream and I looked back to see her lying on the wet floor on her back with arms and legs flailing. My crisis intervention training automatically kicked in assessing the situation as a seizure. I jumped on the woman trying to hold her limbs from hitting equipment then opened her mouth to search for false teeth which might cause her to choke. She punched me hard while yelling, "Get the hell off me you jerk." As it turned out, she simply slipped on the wet floor so all my experience handling seizures was way out of line. I limped back to my office and hid there for the next month.

8

Our family moved back close to our hometown in Massachusetts. We sold our mobile home in New Hampshire and purchased a little home in a nice neighborhood with great friends, school and church. The work stress of dealing with crisis after crisis was replaced with the forward-looking stress of rebuilding a good organization into a great organization. My career attracted regional and national attention which put me on the board and eventually the presidency of the American Hospital Association's Society of Healthcare Education. I started travelling and speaking nationally which put excessive stress on Sandy. She became both mom and dad, focusing on raising the family while I enjoyed the excitement of national exposure. This was a period of selfish excitement on my part while not carrying my share of our marriage.

We still loved each other and married life was great, but we soon found that the excitement of our marriage was becoming tarnished between the demands of family and my traveling nationally. Sandy was a stay-at-home mom and often dad. She also led a Cub Scout troop, served as treasurer of the church's women's program and created crafts for a number of fund-raising projects. I was enrolled in an MBA program and taught management in evening college. Both of us were exhausted at the end of every day, but Sandy was taking the brunt of the workload and stress. Fortunately, a couple of neighbors saw our drifting apart so they suggested a program called Marriage Encounter which was a retreat helping a good marriage to become a great marriage.

We did not want our marriage to suffer so we enrolled in the next Encounter program. It worked by taking us back to that first date of walking Sandy home and our first kiss. We were never not in love, but now we rediscovered the strength which drew us together. But we both had to learn to balance our responsibilities with each other against external demands. To this day, every time I hear the encounter graduation song by the Seekers, "I'll Never Find Another You", I tear up and miss my love with unbelievable hurt. I cannot praise Marriage Encounter enough. Don't wait until your marriage crashes and burns. Find the Encounter weekend and experience how your love began.

My national health care responsibilities kept me busy at home and throughout the country. On every possible occasion I asked Sandy to join me on national trips. Some were better than others but all had the feel of a honeymoon. One trip which almost caused me to lose my mind was a board meeting in Nashville. Sandy and I were able to sneak out to see the sights, but the demands of the board meeting went into the late evening hours to conserve travel expenses. A few of my board members were women who had brought their husbands with them to see Nashville.

At one meal three of the husbands asked Sandy if she wanted to join them in seeing some of the sights while we, on the board, worked into the evening. She agreed and off they went to Music City Row. Our meeting ended around ten or eleven pm and we headed to our rooms. No Sandy, so I called one of my board member's rooms to see if her husband had returned. She said that her husband called her to say Sandy and the three guys were halfway through the music clubs and everything was fine. Great, I fell asleep only to wake up around two am with still no Sandy in our room. Panic set in so I started calling the wives of the husbands who were night clubbing in the after-hours joints in Nashville. No word.

Who unlocks the door at three thirty am but my happy wife who wanted to tell me about the famous entertainers she saw on their all-night excursion.

I was so worried, I was losing my mind and while this completely sober small-town woman wants to tell me about her once in a lifetime exciting evening with three Boy Scout leaders, church-going men who did not drink but wanted to show Sandy the excitement of music city's after-hours clubs.

Sandy put her souvenir cowboy boot glass from Boots Randolph on a prominent shelf in our home just to remind me about love and trust. I still get the shakes every time I see it.

I began picking up my share of home-based activities by coaching our daughter's softball team and jointly helping our son's band program. As our kids moved on to college, we began a joint hobby of beekeeping. Like everything else we did, it soon got out of hand as we could not do anything in a small way. In a short time, we increased to fifty hives which we rented out for pollination. Of course, fifty hives produce a lot of honey so we started a small beekeeping business called Podunk Pollinators for pollination services and New England Honey for honey and hive products. This venture was really fun for both of us as we met crop growers who became good friends.

One old apple grower would meet us with his tractor at nearly ten pm. He would hook his tractor to our flatbed trailer loaded with hives and drive us around his orchard stopping at pallets placed strategically among the trees. Sandy and I jumped off the trailer and placed a hive on his preplaced pallets. Then we opened the entrance of the hive, jumped back on the trailer and on to the next pallet. We would probably finish up around midnight when he would bring us back to his home to be met by his wife and a hot, just out of the oven apple pie which we would enjoy eating while sitting on the stone wall under the stars.

We joined the local beekeeping club where we taught Bee School, a course for people who wanted to start the hobby of beekeeping. This club also set up an exhibit and honey competition at the county fair where we competed in honey, beeswax and baking. Sandy wanted to learn how to prepare items for competition so we vacationed at the University of Nebraska where we learned competitive exhibition methods from their state beekeepers. Sandy was asked by the person who ran the local county fair to enter as many categories as she could to make the booth look full of entries. Of course, the more entries she had, the more ribbons she won.

I began to compete with her but her ribbons made my losing entries look bad. We did not pay attention, but other male beekeepers began grumbling saying that I was preparing her entries, as men always won the ribbons in the past. That was like waving a red flag in front of a bull. Sandy stepped up the quality of her entries and began to win Best of Show and State Ribbons. I loved it as it was like when she was in high school and the guidance person said she couldn't be an accountant. She showed these male beekeepers that they could not compete with her. The result was that many women began entering the competitions and winning more ribbons than the men.

9

In the early 1980's the hospital achieved a leadership status and was ready to begin merger talks with other facilities. Many of us who were the builders had to move on, replaced by those who had the skills of merging organizations. Fortunately, I taught management to a number of business and industrial managers in night school and MBA programs where I gained a comfort in the non-hospital business world. The contacts I made led to a position with a private custom manufacturing company with operations in three states. The owners were getting ready to retire so they wanted to sell to a larger, compatible business. My job was to get the company ready for sale by strengthening the management ranks through training and recruitment. In a short time, we achieved success by being sold to a Swiss multinational which valued my role and kept me on as the HR director for the division. My job was to incorporate a multinational business focus into a private company with a number of business locations across the country. Eventually, I was promoted to manage one of the business locations. My management success resulted in their sending me off for training as a Business Black Belt to help all locations in business improvement. It was all fun but the best part of life was coming home to Sandy to enjoy each other and watch our kids grow.

Our children were grown, completing college and beginning their own lives, marriages and families. Pat graduated as an engineer, but developed a love for finance like her mother so she began working in the field of personal finance. Pat fell in love and married a very nice guy with three young children. Tim graduated as a chemical engineer and began working for a major corporation. He married his college sweetheart. Now they have three wonderful kids. Sandy returned to work when our kids entered public school and became an office manager for an insurance company.

We purchased a larger home to take in our parents should they need to live with family. My parents moved in while Sandy's parents decided to move into a senior housing facility near their friends in Maine. The cycle of life took away our parents, leaving us to focus on our own senior life needs. We built a handicap accessible home on land we owned next to our former home. Our retirements followed and we set out on a journey focusing on each other in our activities of gardening, beekeeping, traveling and relaxing.

Once we were retired, we rediscovered the strength which drew us together. We were able to expand our pollination and honey businesses which we conducted jointly. Travel was now possible due to accumulated airline miles and hotel credits. Sandy and I were able to spend wonderful visits to New Orleans, Las Vegas and locations in Florida. A couple of travel opportunities with groups to Ireland and Scotland provided fun adventures and new friends.

Probably the most exciting opportunity presented to us was when a cousin asked if we wanted to visit Poland and live with a family related to us. The trip was scheduled for six weeks, but we were only able to stay for two. Living with a family in a small rural town in Southern Poland was different and exciting. It seemed like everyone in town had heard about us and knew that my grandmother had grown up there. People took us to her home, which was exactly as she had described it to me as a kid. Of course, the people living in my grandmother's home insisted we stay for a meal with them. Other friends of the folks with whom we were staying invited us to meals at their homes. One day we misunderstood the language and actually had two noon meals scheduled the same day. We were obligated to keep both invitations and had to endure the pleasant pain of the cooks saying, "Eat, eat we made this special for you."

People found my great grandparents' graves in their 400-year-old cemetery. One church group invited us to join a daylong trip visiting a number of shrines and the boyhood home of Pope John Paul. The bus trip was led by their parish priest who led prayers on the beginning of the trip and old drinking songs on the way home. Sandy and my cousin sat with the priest in the front of the bus while her husband and I sat in the rear. The priest began the Hail Mary prayer then began passing the microphone around the front passengers, each saying portions of the prayer in Polish. We knew when the mike was handed to Sandy as all we heard was coughing and sputtering. One of the women saved her by taking the mike to continue the prayer.

Since we were beekeepers, people wanted us to visit a famous beekeeper in the Southern mountains. One of our family members had been a bus driver so he took charge of Sandy and

I traveling south to this mountain apiary. Mr. Nowak, the beekeeper was so happy to have two American beekeepers visit him that he toured us throughout his apiary including a section of antique hives. This trip to Poland will always be remembered for the uniqueness of living with a related family and being invited to the homes of others to share meals and stories.

10

Our life together occasionally had cloudy days, but our first big storm was when Sandy received a diagnosis of breast cancer. Although it was minimized as small, curable with surgery and radiation, it was still cancer with all the fears and threats to our lives and trauma to bring us closer. All the caretakers of cancer treatment were well aware of these threats, so they minimized everything almost to the point of breast cancer being nothing more than a short-term flu. A pleasant surgeon removed tissue saying, "I'm sure I got all of it, but let's do radiation to be sure."

The full month of daily radiation burned Sandy's skin and required frequent applications of cream to reduce the pain. The worst part was the fifteen-mile drive to the clinic every day. She felt every bump in the road and had to cradle her breasts in her arms to minimize the pain. I did the best that I could to avoid bumps and keep the speed slow.

We survived the radiation together and the following year returned to the clinic for the "checkup" mammogram. The technician told Sandy, "Oh my, you have a lot of calcifications and need to have this checked." This technician needed to learn about stress related terms which should not be used with patients.

Sandy went into full panic, fearing a rerun of the surgery and radiation. Of course, the doctor was not much better with his minimizations and reassurances. After spending a good part of my career training medical people in excellence, I wanted to send these "professionals" back to Medical Care 101 to teach them how to talk to real live frightened people. Although we made it through this scare of cancer returning, Sandy never really relaxed.

Within a few months Sandy began feeling tired and fatigued when she began any normal activity. She called for an appointment with her physician, but could only get to see a nurse practitioner. Blood tests were ordered, but showed no abnormalities. The tiredness continued so we again asked to see her physician. This time I sat in on the visit. This doc said it just normal aging, but she probably had sleep apnea and scheduled a sleep test. I mentioned that I had an appointment with my neurologist and would have Sandy join me for that visit.

My doc said that there was no sleep apnea but could not make a diagnosis with this small amount of data. Sandy continued to be too tired to complete normal activities. She could move around the house with a walker but soon had to be helped while walking because of her lack of stability. I became her personal care provider.

Then it happened.

11

One night as we were sleeping Sandy had a major seizure. I felt her shaking violently. I held her and yelled, "Please don't die on me," as I called 911 for an ambulance. The local crew arrived, assessed her and made her ready for transport to the hospital. Her seizure stopped and she was taken into St. Vincent's Hospital. I got dressed and chased the ambulance. The EW staff said that she had another seizure after arriving so they medicated her and admitted her to one of the nursing units. Now began the testing of my poor wife by house staff who I swear wanted to practice procedures in small teaching groups rather than diagnose.

Every time I asked for what was happening to Sandy, they threw up their hands saying, "Nothing conclusive yet." I guess that I finally got a little too demanding as I talked to the nursing staff who recommended that a brain surgeon be called in for a consult. The surgeon explained the brain biopsy procedure and I agreed. He met with me to show the results of the test. Sandy, the love of my life, had a stage 4 glioblastoma which was inoperable. Further, she had about four months to live and hospice was recommended. I was devastated as there was absolutely nothing that I could do to save this person who I had loved for the past sixty-three years.

Sandy was admitted to a hospice and we began notifying family and friends. Her stay did not begin well as our daughter immediately questioned the hospice nurse about whether or not she had read the transfer documents. When Sandy was in the hospital there was a large yellow notice informing the staff that Sandy couldn't swallow so all foods must be pureed. This warning was included in the transfer documents. The hospice served her a plate of chunky scrambled eggs which would have choked her.

The nurse's reply to my daughter was, "We are a hospice and know what we are doing." The nurse finally admitted that the transfer documents were not read, but she complained to her supervisors who demanded to meet with me the next morning. This trio of administrators gave us an ultimatum: an apology from our daughter or Sandy's removal from the facility.

I have to admit that I really wanted to blast their lack of professionalism and their automatically defending their staff over a woman who was emotionally involved with her mother dying. I did my best to calm them down but would not have our daughter apologize. To resolve this, we had a meeting of the minds, but Pat and the floor nurse avoided each other during Sandy's stay. We had to resolve ourselves to the fact that these people did not care for people to help them get better. Instead, they made people comfortable as their lives were ending. Big difference and very difficult, if even possible, for a family to understand and accept.

The hospice social worker gave me a check list of what had to be done to prepare for death. It was the kind of sterile to do list which I wanted to put somewhere and forget about. But our daughter impressed on me the importance of acting on each item. First, a funeral home to prepare Sandy for burial. Sandy had been friends with a funeral director who worked next to her office. She always told me that when she died, she wanted him to take care of her funeral. Pat and I met with this director, who was the first person who really cared about us. As a friend of Sandy, he could not do enough to make our task less difficult. First, he asked what church we would be using. Our church for almost fifty years had a minister who had been so busy getting ready to move on to another church that she did not have time to visit Sandy during her illness. I was so irate over this un-Christian lack of caring that I decided Sandy's service would not be conducted by this person.

Sandy and I had taught the monks of a local monastery how to keep honeybees and actually cared for their hives during one summer when their beekeeper, Brother Adam, developed a serious illness. I called the beekeeping monk to ask if we could use their chapel for the service. They told me that they were not allowed to conduct weddings or funerals in their chapel due to an agreement with area churches. However, they knew Sandy and asked if they could conduct her service if we used the funeral home or a similar facility. The funeral director suggested converting one of his large rooms to a chapel. Sandy would be in an open casket during the service and cremated later for burial in our family plot in Maine.

Sandy had been the treasurer and an active member of her church women's group. Her friends from the group were upset that the church would not be used for the service so a couple of them approached me to ask if they could prepare and serve a luncheon in the church basement following the service at the funeral home. I agreed, as these were her church friends who wanted to show their love for her. Other items on the checklist were insurance notifications, her obituary, and other details on which I reluctantly worked.

In hospice, we spent all our time with Sandy who just lay there quietly, listening to her favorite music, visiting friends and me. The hospice provided compassionate clergy who prayed with us and Sandy alone. She looked like she understood her condition and was resigned to die. Unfortunately, Sandy did not make it the four months the docs had estimated. Instead, she only lived two weeks. Two weeks as that rapid brain cancer took her away from us.

I was alone sitting next to Sandy telling her that I loved her since I first saw her in study hall sixty-three years ago. Our marriage of fifty-five years produced two great kids along with their spouses and six wonderful grandchildren. Sandy listened while moving my hand to massage her knee which had always bothered her. She was unable to talk but could listen and nod. As I spoke to her Pat, our daughter, arrived. We watched her breathing which was taking longer between breaths. I did not want our time to end, but quickly Sandy, the love of my life, took a final deep breath and was gone on the afternoon of June 7, 2018. I did not want her to leave so I kept telling her how much I loved her and that I would meet her again. I kissed her then made the difficult call to the kids to tell them that their mother had passed. Although they saw her failing rapidly, the reality of her death was unacceptable. The hospice staff began their end-of-life rituals which I watched to make sure my wife was treated respectfully. I knew her soul was now with God and her parents in heaven so I left when her friend the funeral director arrived to drive her to the funeral home.

12

Sandy's funeral could not have been more caring, loving and respectful. The service was conducted by our monk friends, attended by family and many friends of both of ours. The room was full of people who wanted to share their memories of Sandy. I could not believe the number and range of people who came to this service to pay their respects and remember Sandy as a friend, neighbor, co-worker, wife, beekeeper, church member and acquaintance. She certainly touched many people. I heard stories of her Cub Scout leadership and girls' softball coaching. People recalled her helping them when she was in the insurance business as well as her years of volunteering to make hundreds of craft projects for her church Christmas Faire. Everyone described her as the nicest person who would quietly help others while presenting the most beautiful smile. Everyone remarked about how much she would be missed and what a chasm would have to be filled by others.

After a parade of "just doing my job" medical staff, I was so happy to be with people who knew and loved Sandy. These expressions of love lasted beyond the after-service reception. I was very proud to have been the husband of such a highly loved and valued person, but every comment heated the pain of my loss to a more intense level. I wanted to scream, "I know, I know, but I lost my whole life." I fought and fought the tears. I just could not cry as I was so angry at everyone and the cancer that ripped Sandy away from the life we were living together.

People must have looked at me and wondered how I could appear so cool and collected when I'd just lost my wife. Little did they know that throughout my life, in every crisis or disaster I had to show this face of cool, collected calm. If I broke the façade everything would fall apart. But, for how long could I hold my breath?

Then it was alone time of painful, silent screaming. I just wanted to escape this world which had grabbed my life away from me. I cannot explain the emptiness when losing someone who shared your life for sixty-three years. It just did not seem real. You sit in the silence believing that the sound you just heard is your love walking into the room. No one can say or do anything helpful. You walk around in a soundless mist not remembering where you are, where you've been, who you've met, what they said and what you were supposed to do. I needed to escape.

Our old camp on a lake in Maine was the perfect place to hide. There was something magical about the place as many of the pleasant things that happened to us happened at this camp. It had become an escape and refuge from many of the life stressors we experienced during our life together. There was just something mystical about sitting on the deck watching the lake, the loons, the eagles and the calming water. The magic of the camp related to many of the revelations and pleasant occurrences that happened to us. So, I packed some food and clothes and escaped to the camp to hide.

On the first day I poured a cup of morning coffee and walked out on the deck to watch the lake. I cannot recall what I thought about or did on the deck, but I remember it getting dark and coming in to bed. I must have sat out there for eight to ten hours with no recall of what if anything I did. But when I went to sleep that night, I slept for the first time in many days. I felt like the day watching the lake washed the anger from me. With no anger to fortify my rigid façade I woke in a bed of tears. From one extreme to another my emotions flowed, but this was a safe place to fall apart as only the loons could watch and join me with their cries of loss.

The next day my daughter called me to remind me to make sure I ate, slept and took care of myself. She also mentioned that while in Maine I had to arrange burial and a service by the local minister. Having family in Maine was a huge help as the local minister said Sandy and I were family so he would be happy to conduct a grave side service. My brother-in-law had already made arrangements to have our stone etched with Sandy's date of death because as he said, "She was my big sister and I wanted to do something for her." He also contacted a friend who would prepare the burial site. A cousin, who was also a bridesmaid at our wedding, wanted to open her home for an after-service gathering where we could all remember the pleasant times and laugh.

During my meeting with the Maine minister, he noticed my red eyes and sensed that I was a basket case so he began counseling me about death of a loved one and the grief that I would feel as I moved forward. He also said that they had a weekly grief group at his church and I would be welcome to attend. I thanked him but said it would be a long way for me to travel weekly. He said that he would then search for a grief group for me closer to my home as I needed to be with others who understood the unstable world I had entered. I really liked this guy. He was not fake or just doing a job. He was going to help me bury my wife here at home among our family. The minister convinced me that this was also a reunion of family who loved each other.

13

Having taken care of most of the checklist items in Maine, one morning I found myself sitting at the local café we had frequented over the years. I ordered breakfast but my staring into space must not have looked like I had it all together so the owner called a friend of Sandy's and mine to come to the restaurant to check on me. Nancy was a distant cousin of Sandy's and frequently joined us for dinner over the years. Nancy and her parents had rented our cabin long before we owned it. Nancy sat across the table from me and must have started small talk but I cannot recall a word.

Weeks later she told me that I was just sitting there, over my breakfast. Nancy was a wonderful, good-hearted person. She retired to Maine from a teaching job in Pennsylvania and has become the "call on me and I will come running to help" hero of this area. She said that we talked but I have no memory of it. After breakfast I was headed home to Massachusetts and I remember Nancy giving me driving advice.

We had planned to have Sandy's burial on August eleventh when all our family could be in Maine. I arrived at the camp a few days early to make sure everything was in order. It was wonderful to see that Sandy's brother Norman had our stone lettered with date of death and had contacted a friend to dig the grave for the container of ashes. Linda, one of Sandy's bridesmaids, arranged to have an after burial gathering at her home. I met with the minister to tell him some personal information about Sandy as he knew our family but not us, as we lived out of state. He again emphasized that I could really benefit from a grief group so he would locate a group close to my home in Massachusetts.

Nancy checked on me and offered to take me to lunch to just relax and talk. I don't remember what we talked about, but it was pleasant to spend time with an old friend who knew Sandy and me. There was something comfortable about reminiscing about Sandy and the pain of our loss. It was like Nancy caught me during a disastrous fall into a dark hole with no bottom. I wanted to spend more time with her. She was warm, comforting and supportive.

The graveside service was beautiful. It was a nice day and we were surrounded by family and friends not only in attendance, but in nearby family graves. Sandy's mother and father's graves were next to her along with Sandy's uncles and their wives. Across the path was her grandmother Lil and grandfather Guy who raised Sandy while her father and mother were stationed in Norfolk, Virginia during WWII. I did not want to leave the love of my life in that graveyard on a hill in Maine, but since she would be back among family she loved, it was comforting.

Our granddaughter, Sophia, sang "Bright Blue Rose," a favorite from our travels to Ireland. I came back to the graveyard after everyone left to ask our family buried there to watch over Sandy while I left for home. But, on every trip to Maine I visit Sandy and transplant her favorite flowers from her garden.

The rest of that summer and fall I spent a lot of time in Maine visiting Sandy's grave because I missed her so much. On every trip Nancy and I would have lunch or just ride around the back roads to talk and remember my Sandy. A person cannot live through grief alone so Nancy was a godsend. It's really cruel how many people considered grief to be a three-day experience. Their comments like, "You'll feel better soon," or "She had a great life," or "You'll meet someone new," or the worst one, "Soon you will forget her," made me feel worse, in spite of their intentions. Nancy was not judgmental, just a calming presence, sharing good memories.

Nancy's brother lived in Massachusetts so when she visited him, she stayed at our house to sort through Sandy's clothes for donation. During the following year we met more often in Maine and Massachusetts, enjoying each other's company. Nancy even asked me to drive down to the Pennsylvania with her to meet her children. All seemed to be going very well as two old friends talking on the phone, visiting each other and maybe even falling in love.

14

Our home was the loneliest place I've ever been with Sandy gone. Even her cat Skittles just kept walking around looking for her. I intentionally left her clothes and papers out where she had last left them, dreaming that Sandy would come walking through the door any minute. The rest of that summer and fall I spent a lot of time in Maine transplanting some of her favorite flowers from home to keep her company.

We did not plan to fall in love and it was too soon after Sandy's passing to be even thinking about a relationship. This just snuck up on us as the three of us had been friends for years. It's hard to explain, but when Nancy and I were together, it seemed like Sandy was also there like in the old days. I'm sure it's crazy and there must be some sort of psychological explanation, but Nancy and I entered this zone of comfort without realizing it.

Reality appeared when we got too close to each other without Sandy. We talked about the idea of moving in together, but that may be where the light of reality began to illuminate the relationship. We were not kids trying to plan thirty or forty years together. We were both in our seventies, each with a lifetime's collection of baggage which did not seem to fit in an unimaginable short future together. So, we both became surprised and embarrassed at how our relationship had changed.

We began to argue more maybe to create distance between us. We both developed any number of reasons to support a parting of ways and a return to our individual lives. I'm sure both of us left with good feelings for each other which were overshadowed by our individual stubbornness.

We have not spoken since the breakup as not everyone lives happily ever after. My loss of Nancy was devastating. I had not only lost Sandy, the love of my life since childhood, but I now lost Nancy, a very dear old friend who saved my life when I was drowning in grief. What more loss could I experience?

15

Sandy's best friend at church, Mabel, entered hospice care at her home due to a serious lung condition a few months after Sandy passed. Mabel had made a prayer shawl for Sandy. This shawl became a piece of her world that she held tight until she died. Mabel was not only a friend of Sandy's from church, but she was a nurse in the same hospital where I had worked. Our friendship called me to visit her in hospice. Other nurses joined us and the visits became a great delight for Mabel. She wanted us to retell all those funny stories from our hospital work nights.

Her favorite story concerned the day Sandy and I were skating with our kids and I fell on the ice resulting in a concussion. I was transported to the hospital and held overnight for observation. About two am Mabel and a couple of fellow staff from her unit came into my room playing "The Skaters Waltz" on combs covered with waxed paper. These great night shift musicians were called the Silver Comb Band who practiced in the med closet during breaks. She asked us to tell that story over and over during her hospice time. Mabel would laugh and laugh asking to tell more stories again and again. We worried about her catching her breath and turned her oxygen concentration as high as possible to keep her from gasping. Too quickly Mabel passed away and I suffered from another loss of a dear companion.

The promise of the minister in Maine to find me a grief group to join became a reality. I joined a local Baptist church group which met every Sunday evening. I thought that I could keep myself composed while listening to advice on how to handle grief. Little did I know that at my first meeting I would be asked to introduce myself and talk about who I lost. I began strong talking about the beautiful fourteen-year-old girl I sat behind in study hall, but began to choke while talking about our time in hospice, then I fell apart talking about the additional loss of Mabel within a few months of Sandy. Fortunately, the group gathered around my inability to talk about love lost.

I stayed and benefitted from this grief group, but had difficulty understanding the Biblical answers to every question. If someone asked, "How long will I feel like this?" the answer was always a reference from the Bible with which I had no familiarity. I found comfort with this group, but not the ability to work through my grief without reading and knowing the Bible.

I think the event that hurt me the most and caused me to leave the group was the time we were having a discussion about our loved one's death. A number of people mentioned that their loved one died in accidents or alone without opportunity for anyone to say "I love you," or "Goodbye". I felt bad for those folks so when it became my turn to talk, I expressed sorrow for the way they lost their loved ones without any final words. I told them that I was so fortunate to spend time in hospice where all the I love you's and goodbye's could be expressed. I was interrupted by a woman who said a hospice is a place of murder where spouses are forced to pull the plug on a loved one. Despite my words, she strongly felt that the medical people forced her to kill her husband by removing life support. This woman was not ready for grief discussions as her feelings of guilt were much too raw.

At the same time other people in the group began saying that they belonged to this grief group for five or seven years and answered her in matter-of-fact statements like, "You'll get over it," and "Just wait until you have been here as long as us." This grief group started to feel like a perpetual grievers anonymous group dominated by the long termers. I just could not feel comfortable in this group any longer so I thanked everyone and said my goodbyes. Now what was I going to do? It seemed like I was moving from one losing situation to another. What was I doing wrong? Although I did not know much about the Bible, one statement that I heard in the grief group kept haunting me.

"I have made you. I will carry you; I will sustain you and I will rescue you." (Isaiah 46:4)

I'm not a big religious guy but this statement kept rolling around in my head. Perhaps someone was looking after me during this period of loss. Coincidentally, Brother Adam, a monk at the abbey and close friend of ours, called to say he had found a grief group at St. Mary's Church which would be starting shortly. Adam said that some of his relatives were members of St. Mary's so I would be welcomed. This became an offer I could not refuse so I called Vi, the group leader to ask if I could join. Her answer, "Of course, it was all arranged thanks to Brother Adam."

So, I drove one hour to Shrewsbury to join the group. Along with two other members, Hadar and Mary Ellen, I was welcomed with hugs and a prayer. The group leaders Vi and Corrine had led previous groups so they knew how uncomfortable we were and how easily we could relax with their leadership. Unlike my previous group this was a low-key structured experience designed to help us move through the elements of grief with the goal of being able to accept, cope and move on in our lives, building on the good memories of our lost loved ones. For the first time I felt comfortable being in a grief group. Weeks later we would remark on becoming a family of five who focused on understanding and helping each other.

Our grief group finished the structured program with each of us feeling an inner strength to move us forward. But as we discovered, moving through grief requires the companionship of others who can jump in when a trigger brings to life some of the emotional feelings. The two leaders said that there was something unique about this group of five that formed a supportive family bond which still exists today. We text each other, meet for lunch and stay close to each other as a close family would.

16

We all kept building on the structure of the program and improving with group support. Then COVID raised its ugly head and hit us pretty hard with two of our family testing positive, and two of us requiring testing and fifteen-day quarantines. Our family could no longer meet in person, but thanks to social media, we continued to stay in touch and support each other. It is very difficult to deal with grief alone and this COVID panic demanded isolation. As a family, we were determined to constantly check on each other and watch sports and other programs while making comments to each other via texting.

The member who had a long hospital stay was our Villanova grad and a Nova men's basketball fan. She and I would watch the games, she in her hospital room and me at home. I always took the opposing team and we would text each other all during the game. It was fun as she was Nova's number one fan, but couldn't have visitors. She really enjoyed the trash talk after every basket as it took her mind off her medical problems.

I suffered another loss which seemed like it was happening on the other side of the world because we were not allowed to physically be there to process it. My granddaughter who, due to her illness, could not cope with the COVID driven isolation, took her life. That was devastating as funerals were limited, travel restricted and family mourning almost nonexistent due to governmental mandates. The absolute insanity of this pandemic prevented us from grieving our loved ones through wakes, funerals and burials. Many families suffered from COVID driving us to isolation.

Our grief group could not meet for lunch so we celebrated online the fact that we were able to cope and not be consumed by isolation and loneliness. Hadar, one of our members who was Jewish, circulated a video of Rabbi Manis Friedman explaining how the COVID isolation was causing the world to shut down. He reminded us that our worlds of work, school, theater, shopping and other activities were now gone so what would we do? How would we react? Would some ignore the warning and just push on as if nothing changed? Would others get into a fetal position to fall into depression?

He suggested COVID presented tremendous opportunity to focus on those activities we never had the time to address. Read, write, exercise and play with the kids. If physical love was worrisome, how could we increase affection without touching? Most importantly, how could we help and serve others in our neighborhoods and communities without physical contact? Rabbi Friedman asked us to breathe life into life by getting closer to God to search for ways we could use the isolation for growth and improvement.

I was blown away by this idea of making a bad situation good by changing the focus from a problem to an opportunity. COVID news was devastating as each day brought more depressing stories of numbers of people with the virus and stories of individuals dying without contact with their loved ones. These sad stories demanded periods of mourning. But as the rabbi said, mourn but save time to quietly give thanks for that which we are grateful and find opportunities for growth and resetting life. He also said to listen during the silence of isolation for God's soft voice providing guidance for the path forward. I kept hearing those words from Isaiah:

"I have made you. I will carry you; I will sustain you and I will rescue you."

17

I searched social media and found old friends I had worked with throughout my career. What wonderful surprises these on-line meetings provided in reminiscing about those experiences which made differences to our lives many years ago. Everyone was starved for some relief from the loss of their worldly activities. Everyone wanted to reminisce about the fun and the good times. One friend, Jo-Ann, reappeared after forty years to send me a photo of a small duck decoy which I carved for her as a gift when we worked together in the 1980's.

The nuggets of memory which we all keep are wonderful remembrances years later when we have trouble recognizing our aged images. We all discovered the memories which were important to hold on to and now relived them as if they had occurred yesterday. We may have been isolated but we were not alone. We not only talked about our pasts, we shared our present situations and reassured each other about our futures. Jo-Ann was now retired and living in Florida. We began texting and calling each other to reminisce and fill in our lives over the forty years since we worked together.

Another friend, Candace from Minnesota, ran the customer service department of our operation there. She reminded me of the running joke we had about that state fair food fried fish on a stick. When I led management meetings at their location,

I would always joke about the big treat at the state fair; the fish—walleye— cooked and placed on a stick like an ice cream bar. After one meeting everyone in the room held up paper walleyes on sticks to remind me that the meeting was almost as good as this state fair treat.

Social media also reintroduced friends who had passed on. Stanley Urban was my best friend in high school and he and his band played for Sandy's and my wedding reception. Stan had a successful business career then traded it all to purchase a couple of hotels in Haiti. We met him at a high school reunion and Stan did everything he could to convince Sandy and I to come to Haiti to visit him. Unfortunately, life's rush of activities gave us excuses not to make the trip. I regret that now.

I remembered another friend when I read her obituary. Robin was our corporate nurse who had to make periodic visits to our business sites around the country. Since I also had to travel the circuit Robin often asked if she could travel with me, making it safer than a woman traveling alone. Robin's and my favorite site was Grand Prairie Texas because there was this little old black grandmother who ran the best BBQ in the state. Her name was Momma Crown and her BBQ was in an old two bay automotive garage with a collection of yard sale 1950's chrome kitchen tables and chairs, none of which matched. Momma and her two grandsons ran the business by loading the giant cement block smoker at five am with whatever she could buy reasonably—brisket, hot links, pork butt, chicken, ribs and anything else available. She opened the smoker at eleven am to a line of people patiently waiting.

I was usually in line on Fridays and if Momma saw me, she would yell, "Hey Boston, got your jug?" I would get a clean one-gallon sample jug from the plant and Momma would fill it with whatever she had then added a jar of her BBQ sauce. I would put it in a sealed taped box to contain the smoke smell and carry it on the plane and home Friday night for Sandy to enjoy.

When Robin visited Momma Crown's with me, she would yell out hello to Momma who she claimed was a twin to her own grandmother. Momma would ask Robin, "What can I make for you that your grandmother made?" One time Robin said she wished she could taste her grandmother's apple fritters again. Momma said, "I'll have them ready when you finish lunch," then proceeded to pour a mound of flour on the workbench. In no time fresh apple fritters were coming out of the fryer and served to Robin. I really miss Robin's laugh and company on these business trips. She would tell great stories about her son and husband and their absolute addiction to NASCAR racing.

It was absolutely amazing how uplifting these reminiscences and reunions with old friends could be. It really felt like wedges of warm light sneaking in through the cracks in the wall of this dungeon I had been living in. If I could not interact with old friends, I read inspiring books and articles about positive spiritual growth. It did not matter what the religion of the author was as all are related in their presentations of good and bad, negative and positive. The comforting thing for me was the belief that the Gods they talk about do not sit on some pinnacle granting wishes. Rather, God resides in your heart and is always present to hear your prayers.

One example of this is Sufism which talks about the three voices that speak to us. One is the voice of darkness which always comes up with the worst possible outcomes. The second is the voice of self which is the file cabinet of all the good and bad beliefs and prejudices which forces a behavior based only on these learned responses. The third voice is the voice of the Divine or sometimes called the voice of God. It is the voice from your heart unaffected by voices of self and darkness. Although I did not recognize it as the three voices of Sufism when I was a business manager wrestling with a major decision affecting people, I now realize that my best decisions, most appreciated by coworkers were those from my heart.

18

I needed to practice mindfulness and the quieting of the voices of darkness and self-doubt because COVID was so devastating as each day brought more depressing news. People no longer had names and faces. Instead, all we heard were numbers of people with the virus and stories of groups dying without contact with their loved ones. These sad stories demanded periods of mourning. But as the rabbi said, mourn but save time to quietly give thanks for that in which we are grateful. The gratefulness will help us to float above the sewer of COVID. Further, he reminded us to keep listening during the silence for God's soft voice providing guidance for the path forward. I kept hearing those words from Isaiah: *"I have made you. I will carry you; I will sustain you and I will rescue you."*

I could not believe that I was actually stepping away from the lonely pain of loss and solitary confinement to listen for the softness of God's voice providing steps forward through this storm. I heard rest, eat healthy, reach out to friends, read, pray, become active and learn how to dance in the rain as no one can see your tears. I heard, felt and received God's grace as a one-sided coin. The coin does not flip grace or no grace. Grace always comes up on a one-sided coin. My actions and searches were always positive because of God's grace.

As I searched social media, I bumped into more interesting people willing to share themselves on a range of topics. While searching for recipes for one-person meals, I bumped into Brenda Gantt, who invited us into her kitchen via Facebook to watch and listen to her prepare homemade meals mostly for herself. She was a retired school teacher living alone in Andalusia, Alabama, but with an army of friends. Brenda was a good religious woman who often introduced us to other positive people from her community and church.

One such person was Jan White who wrote a regular column of every day faith for a local Andalusia newspaper. Jan had combined eighty of her columns in a book titled "Everyday Faith for Daily Life." As she described her stories, I knew that I had to read and learn from her work so I immediately ordered her book. What a wonderful surprise it was. In my Baptist grief group, I had great difficulty reading and understanding the Bible, but Jan's collection of stories were about real people living out their lives of faith based on Biblical lessons. I read, learned and enjoyed her work then decided to contact her for advice about how I might move through my grief and COVID isolation with the assistance of the soft voice of God.

Jan's advice was simple. She said that often people overlook those little, but powerful things which happen during each day. These small, pleasant occurrences are often overshadowed by the daily worries, disappointments and failures. The power of the little positive things comes from recognizing, accumulating and being grateful for each one. Jan said that when you identify and collect these small, positive experiences, they will change your life. Her suggestion was that at the end of each day, no matter how good or bad it is, I should write down those few things for which I am grateful to have experienced. It could be as simple as a hot cup of coffee, someone's smile or a personal accomplishment.

I began this bedtime exercise with some difficulty. Sunny day today; good lunch; peaceful afternoon nap. However, the surprising thing was that at the end of each day things began to stand out as items I enjoyed and benefitted from experiencing. Not only was I remembering things to be grateful for, but I was ending each day on a positive note. I was falling asleep not with a worry or a major upset, but with pleasant, positive experiences. This gratefulness list must have started making a difference in wellbeing as I began to sleep better without the worried wake-ups.

I began my mornings more excited about the day ahead. I think that I may even started hunting for positive experiences rather than fretting about failures or worries. Jan was correct. If you count those things for which you are grateful, you will begin to search for those experiences and actually change your outlook on life from negative or depressed to a positive search for beneficial experiences each day, like using a one-sided coin.

I read a message by Oprah Winfrey which said, "Being grateful all the time isn't easy. But it's when you feel least thankful that you are most in need of what gratitude can give you: perspective. Gratitude can transform any situation. It alters your vibration, moving you from negative energy to positive. It's the quickest, easiest, most powerful way to effect change in your life – this I know for sure."

In just a couple of weeks, gratefulness began a cycle of success for me. I was able to feel the positive energy. This wasn't my imagination or a rose-colored glasses approach. Rather it was a refocusing from negatives to positives in every day by listing those things for which I was grateful. You don't eliminate the negatives, but they just don't monopolize your time and drag you down. I began the daily gratefulness exercise shortly after the beginning of the COVID pandemic and now after a couple of years of listing those experiences, I am much happier. I look forward to the five minutes sitting on the side of the bed jotting down five to ten things which happened that day and for which I am grateful. Each entry may be only a few words but is allows me to relive and enjoy the experience before I fall asleep. I have to admit on some days my grateful list is short and hard to recall because the negatives were too strong, but that is a rare occurrence. Each day is like a painting on canvas with some paintings just not having the right colors.

19

Today, I have difficulty being negative about life as I was just after Sandy died. My daily canvases look a lot brighter. I no longer feel the guilt of not having been able to save the life of my love. I no longer hate my life without her or feel useless. As Jan said, this simple brief habit will change your world from negative to positive. All you need is that empty notebook in the drawer and a pen to paint tomorrow's empty canvas.

Jan did not leave me with just the important message of gratitude. In recognizing my limited religious knowledge, she recommended that I learn more about God and the beautiful statement in John about Jesus, "The word became flesh." Jan told me about a New York Times best-selling author, Max Lucado, who translates specific portions of the Bible into understandable books which read like short stories. She recommended two books for me to begin my learning: "No Wonder They Call him the Savior," and "Six Hours One Friday," about the final hours of Christ. Both were powerful and realistic works whetting my appetite for more. I read more of Lucado's books and the book of John in a modern English translation of the Bible. My readings became supported with daily social media messages of reinforcement. Bishop Robert Barron translates a short Gospel into lay terms. A group of women religious writers post everyday trials and tribulation readings and prayers for, but not limited to, women under the title of Your Daily Prayer. I also read daily postings from Jewish and Sufi teachers.

Not only was I learning about God's love, grace and kindness, but everything was beginning to make sense. Throughout my life I perceived religion as what we see in the rituals, and beliefs of separation, probably learned from early religious turmoil in my family. It was always good vs. bad, mine vs. yours, heads vs. tails. To me, religion looked like a two-sided coin. However, everything I was learning and experiencing demonstrated that no matter the religious affiliation, God is the center of it all and grace is a one-sided coin. What a wonderful feeling of accomplishment, peace and gratitude.

Now that I felt ready to face the world, my friends became even more supportive. I had known many people throughout my life and several them started appearing in front of me on Facebook, in text messages, and even referrals from other friends. I cannot explain the magic of these occurrences, but something was happening to reconnect these friends to me perhaps—God's grace.

20

A couple of my reacquainted friends reminded me of the person I was years earlier compared to who I am today. With Sandy's passing I lost some of who they knew and enjoyed so they helped begin my reconstruction. With their help we identified four attributes I possessed in the past which people valued. I was respected. I was caring. I was giving. I was grateful. My friends and I agreed that this is who I was with Sandy's loving support, and this is who I must become with Sandy's love and memories. One friend said, "When we lose that person we love, we must not learn to live without them, rather to live with the love they left behind." We all talked about Sandy and the love she shared to make us the people we became. For me, I go forward expressing these attributes expressed in these affirmations this way:

I am a worthy person; worthy of being happily involved, loved and respected.

I am a loving person who reaches out to others in sincere, caring ways.

I am a giving person who helps, volunteers and shares myself with others without expectations.

I am a grateful person who is overwhelmed by and very appreciative of the gifts I have received and the people who have shared themselves with me.

I printed these affirmations on a card and taped it to the back of my cellphone as a constant reminder of who I was, who Sandy married, and who my friends said I needed to find and reveal to myself and the world. In essence, this was a rediscovery of self, a comfort with the rediscovery and a love of self. As I gain more and more self-confidence, I am able to climb out of the crater and demolition of loss, to move into a new life built of all the loving experiences of the past. Nothing ever leaves you. You remember the happiness as well as the pain. But through the power of gratitude and friends I rediscovered who I was and who I am becoming. I am moving into a new life thanks to God's grace.

I am now not only able to be comfortable with myself, but I am able to love and to rebuild my life with God's soft voice guiding me on the path forward. As I begin each day the first thing I do is to greet God and give thanks for waking to another day. In anticipating positive experiences, I thank God for the path he has laid out for me, and I ask for help in moving ahead in life with Sandy's love and memories. At the end of each day, I spend five minutes on the edge of my bed remembering and listing in a notebook those things for which I am grateful that day. For a person who was not very religious I am overwhelmed with how simple and loving God's grace can be in one's life. God's grace is a one-sided coin. God provides grace in place of grace already given, (John 1:15) always landing face side up as a one-sided coin.

Epilogue

For a guy who did not have much religious teaching or any familiarity with the Bible, I have started enjoying a podcast by Father Mike Schmitz who is presenting the Bible in daily twenty minute very interesting readings. My experiences are spiritual and not confined to a single religious following. My experiences involve Protestants, Catholics, Jews, and Sufis. However, the commonality is God, as a soft voice in our hearts.

I am sure that some people will explain my transition through grief and isolation as indoctrination or born-again salvation or even some sort of psychological phenomena. I really do not care what people think or conclude. I'm not trying to convince anyone of anything. I lost my life when Sandy died but some powerful graceful force rescued, carried and directed me through experiences which helped me to rebuild a new life on the foundation of Sandy's love. Somewhere I saw a sign saying, "God, I can't handle this" with the "I Can't" crossed out. God handled it for me and I am forever grateful.

All the people I met, read or texted with, referred to a God who does not sit on a mountain somewhere waiting to grant us favors. God is with us constantly in our hearts talking to us in a soft voice of comfort, love, inspiration and grace. We can easily miss all this if we do not create enough quiet in the hurricane of loss to hear his voice. That Rabbi who said that the isolation of COVID will stop all activity to create enough quiet to hear God was correct. I heard God's soft voice telling me how to move on the path forward. He helped me to become more positive through gratitude. I enjoyed the laughter and memories with friends. I learned to accept, value and love myself instead of dwelling on the blame and hate which eats us alive when we lose the most important loved one in our lives.

I don't know what God has in store for me further down this path. I do know that I am eighty years old and the path ahead gets shorter with every step. I also realize that my life has changed dramatically by just listening to a soft, grace-filled voice. I discovered that God's grace is a one-sided coin. I know that this path will take me home. I hear a soft voice saying to me, "I have a place for you right beside this woman with the beautiful jet-black ponytail."

Acknowledgements

This memoir began with a simple request from the leaders of a grief support group for me to write a few words of loving memory of my wife Sandy. I am indebted to Vi Jefferson and Corrine Hetzler for their request and to Mary Ellen Costa and Hadar Philbin for sharing their grief and support. Members of my writing group Amy Paul, and Ed Londergan encouraged me to write more about my wife. MaryAnne Slack edited my words with empathy, expertise and unending patience. My daughter Patricia Shermeta and daughter in law Jennifer Metcalf offered support, editing and book design. Kasey Rogers, a recent memoir author guided me through formatting and entering the publishing world.

What began as a grief exercise moved me through the remembering, writing and emotion of this memoir always, constantly motivated by a soft voice of God saying that there are others with the same pain who could benefit from the path offered to me.

www.ingramcontent.com/pod-product-compliance
Lightning Source LLC
Chambersburg PA
CBHW021012180726
47993CB00019B/2705